W9-AYD-075

How Things Are Made

Wax to Crayons

By Inez Snyder

Welcome Books™

Children's Press®
A Division of Scholastic Inc.
New York / Toronto / London / Auckland / Sydney
Mexico City / New Delhi / Hong Kong
Danbury, Connecticut

Thanks to the staff of R&F Handmade Paints, Kingston, NY

Photo Credits: Cover and all photos by Cindy Reiman
Contributing Editor: Jennifer Silate
Book Design: Mindy Liu

Library of Congress Cataloging-in-Publication Data

Snyder, Inez.
  Wax to crayons / by Inez Snyder.
  p. cm. — (How things are made)
  Includes index.
  Summary: An introduction to the process by which wax is transformed into crayons.
  ISBN 0-516-24267-9 (lib. bdg.) — ISBN 0-516-24359-4 (pbk.)
  1. Crayons—Juvenile literature. [1. Crayons.] I. Title. II. Series.

TS1268 .S649 2003
741.2'3—dc21   2002009375

Copyright © 2003 by Rosen Book Works, Inc.
All rights reserved. Published simultaneously in Canada.
Printed in China.
16 R 15

Contents

Crayons are made from **wax**.

First, the wax is heated.

Wax **melts** when it is hot.

Colored **powder** is mixed into the hot wax.

The wax becomes the same color as the powder.

Next, the colored wax
is put into a **mold**.

The mold will make the wax
in the shape of crayons.

When the wax cools,
it becomes hard.

The hard wax is taken
out of the mold.

The wax is now in the
shape of crayons.

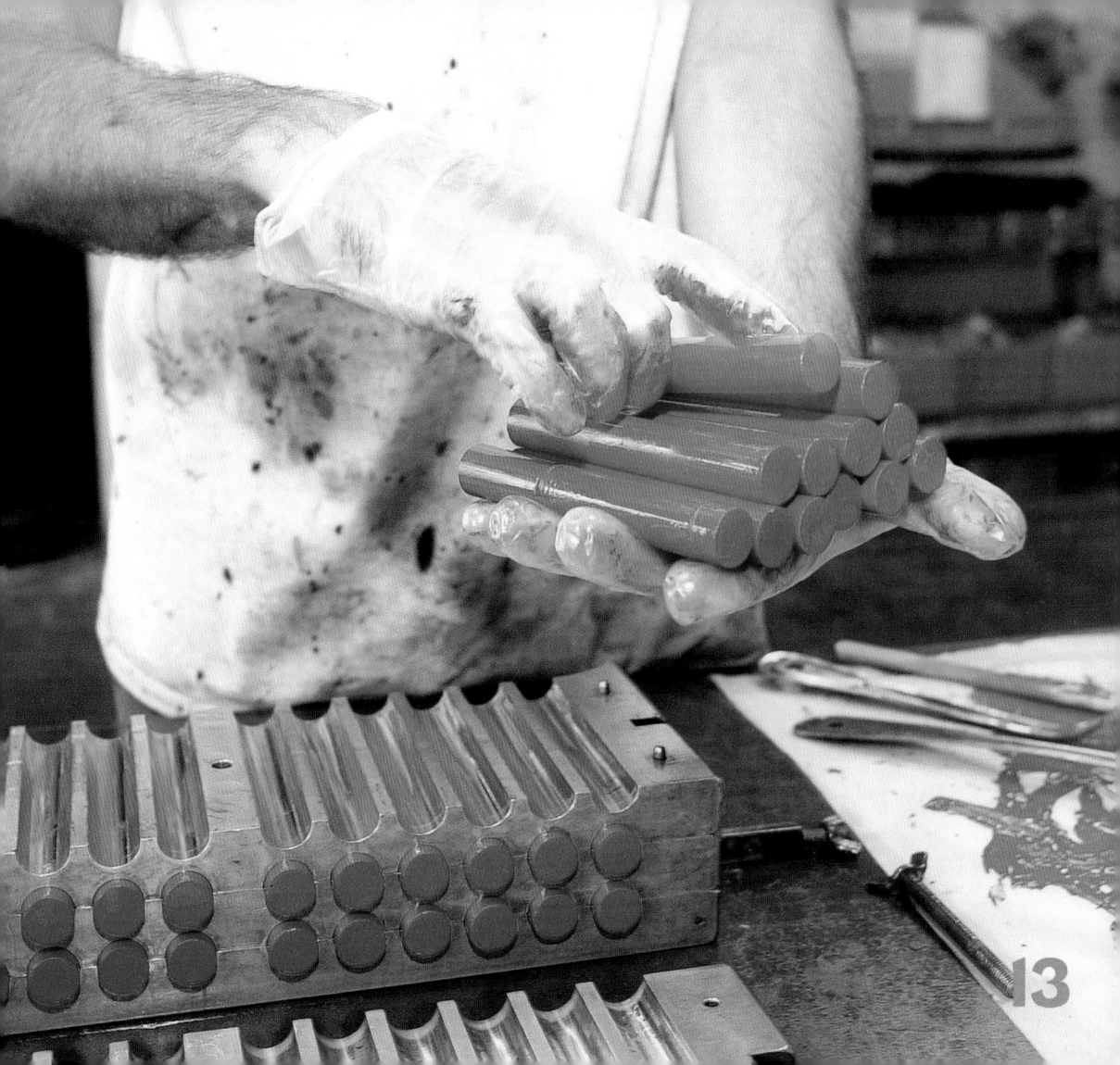

A worker looks at the crayons.

He makes sure the crayons are not broken.

Then, someone puts **labels** on each crayon.

The finished crayons
are put into boxes.

Now, the crayons are
ready to be used.

We use crayons to draw and color on paper.

Crayons are fun to use.

New Words

crayons (**kray**-uhnz) colored wax sticks used
for drawing or coloring

labels (**lay**-buhlz) pieces of paper that are
attached to something and give information

melts (**melts**) goes from being solid to
being liquid

mold (**mohld**) a hollow container that you can
pour liquid into so that it sets in that shape

powder (**pou**-dur) tiny particles of a solid
substance

wax (**waks**) a substance made from fats or oils

To Find Out More

Books
Crayons: From Start to Finish
by Samuel G. Woods
Gale Group

From Wax to Crayon
by Michael H. Forman
Children's Press

Web Site
Crayola Kids
http://www.crayola.com/kids/index.cfm
Play games, color pictures, and take a tour through the
Crayola factory on this Web site.

Index

About the Author

Inez Snyder writes and edits children's books. She also enjoys painting and cooking for her family.

Reading Consultants

Kris Flynn, Coordinator, Small School District Literacy, The San Diego County Office of Education

Shelly Forys, Certified Reading Recovery Specialist, W.J. Zahnow Elementary School, Waterloo, IL

Sue McAdams, Former President of the North Texas Reading Council of the IRA, and Early Literacy Consultant, Dallas, TX